I0669694

Edward Jerningham

The Fall of Mexico

A Poem

Edward Jerningham

The Fall of Mexico
A Poem

ISBN/EAN: 9783744712668

Printed in Europe, USA, Canada, Australia, Japan

Cover: Foto ©Thomas Meinert / pixelio.de

More available books at **www.hansebooks.com**

THE

FALL OF MEXICO,

A

POEM.

By Mr. JERNINGHAM.

LONDON:
PRINTED BY SCOTT,
FOR J. ROBSON, BOOKSELLER, NEW BOND STREET.
MDCCLXXV.

ADVERTISEMENT.

GUATIMOZINO, the laſt emperour of MEXICO, having oppoſed the SPANIARDS with great bravery, in various engagements, was at length defeated and taken priſoner. In order to extort from him a diſcovery of the principal mines, he was laid on burning coals; The ſecond in command was alſo condemn'd to the ſame torture, and amidſt his ſufferings called upon his royal maſter to be releaſed from the vow of ſecrecy, which drew from GUATIMOZINO theſe memorable words: *Am I on a Bed of Roſes?*

DRYDEN has put theſe words into the mouth of MONTEZUMA contrary to the teſtimony of the hiſtorians.

THE

FALL OF MEXICO.

THE Sun now glitter'd in the front of day,
And wide-diffuſing his reſplendent ray,
Look'd willing to adorn the glorious meed,
The realm!—To GUATIMOZINO decreed!
Whom for his valour tried and virtue known,
His country's voice invited to the throne.

Now, thro' th' applauding clamour of the throng,
Th' auguſt proceſſion ſlowly mov'd along,
While in the rear of this progreſſive ſcene,
Endearing ſight! the choſen Youth was ſeen,

Rais'd on a lofty ſeat of burniſh'd gold,
Which twelve illuſtrious Mexicans uphold.

The law ordain'd a ſignal to diſplay
The function, mode, and colour of the day:
A ſplendid ſtreamer playing to the view,
(Inwrought with plumage of celeſtial blue)
Mark'd from the ſummit of a lofty tow'r,
Of Joy's great feſtival the leading hour:
This maſter-ſign the diſtant flag obey'd,
And prompt alike the glad report convey'd,
Which poſting on the rapid wings of ſight,
To ev'ry city urg'd its ſpeedy flight,
Till Mexico throughout her vaſt extent
Burſt into joy with one declar'd aſſent!

Behold the ſolemn ſlow-advancing train
Approach the precincts of the ſacred fane;
A venerable, rude, majeſtic pile,
Of time remote, which claim'd the ſtubborn toil:

By gloomy Fancy on the portal plann'd,
Bold from the ſculptor's all-creative hand,
Full many a wild terrific image ſprung:
There angry ſerpents intertwining hung:
There the God's agent, Terrour! fond to dwell,
Breath'd all around his awe-diffuſing ſpell.

See now the train the ſpacious dome receive,
Where clouds of fragrance circling altars heave!
Four golden columns with bright jaſper crown'd,
The hallow'd image of the God ſurround.
Now from his ſeat the choſen Youth deſcends,
And to that image prompt his footſteps bends,
Where ANDALUSIA, form'd in Beauty's mould,
And high on Virtue's ſacred liſt enroll'd,
With fear, with love, with baſhful youth impreſs'd,
Expecting ſtood the bride of his requeſt.

"Deign to partake, th' illuſtrious chieftan ſaid,
"The growing honours that around me ſpread;

" Consent the glory of a throne to share,
" Be thine the pleasure, and be mine the care."

Lo at their side the priest TALEPO stands,
And joins, in wedlock's tie, their willing hands:
Then rearing to the view th' imperial crown,
The pontiff said: " Thou fav'rite of renown,
" Warm in whose breast each kindred virtue lives,
" Behold the glorious meed thy country gives!
" The trembling hand which late to thine I join'd,
" Is as the pledge of her love-glowing mind,
" So is this crown the thronging votes impart,
" The sacred token of thy country's heart.
" The radiant wisdom to thy birth allied,
" Thy valour in the field of danger tried,
" Thy sympathy that wakes at Sorrow's sigh,
" These are the charms that glitter in her eye!
" Thy valour rushing as th' impetuous stream,
" (Ah let me linger on th' enchanting theme)

" Impell'd thee to reſiſt the foreign hoſt,
" That pour their numbers on our wond'ring coaſt,
" And hurl'd, like Gods, deſtructive thunders round!
" Alarm'd, aſtounded at th' unuſual ſound,
" Our archers hurried from th' unequal fight,
" And urg'd precipitate their trembling flight;
" While female ſhrieks, and children's piercing cries,
" With mix'd diſcordance, iſſued to the ſkies.
" 'Twas then, amid this univerſal fear,
" That thou, undaunted, did'ſt thy valour rear,
" And as the rock that checks the torrent's roll,
" Ev'n ſo did'ſt thou the flying throng control,
" And on each archer's breaſt, to terrour prone,
" Did'ſt pour the warm effuſions of thy own:
" Charm'd by the ſpell of thy enliv'ning word,
" They face the daring foe with one accord;
" With thee the terrours of the combat brave,
" And make th' extenſive coaſt one SPANISH grave.
" For this thy country decks thee with renown,
" And fixes on thy brow this ſplendid crown."

He ceas'd——while thro' the wide extending fane
The voice of Gladneſs pours her plauſive ſtrain.

Lo! now, an herald comes with ſpeedy pace,
His thought expanding o'er th' expreſſive face:
Feſtivity reſigns her ſhort-liv'd charms,
While loud he cries—" To arms—To arms—To arms!
" Proud of their daring, an alarming hoſt
" Of warring SPANIARDS darken all the coaſt:
" High-rais'd on beings of ſuperior force,
" They urge reſiſtleſs their deſtructive courſe:
" Their chieftan's voice theſe monſters well obey,
" Fierce they purſue where he directs the way!
" Babes, mothers, men, are in one carnage trod,
" By theſe new engines of that demi-God!"

" Hail to th' event, the new-crown'd youth returns,
" To meet theſe foes my panting boſom burns:"
Then to the beauteous bride, o'erwhelm'd with grief,
With plaintive voice applied the royal chief:

" The joy expectancy had painted high,
" And bath'd in all the colours of the ſky,
" Flies like the bird who deck'd with ev'ry hue,
" Wings gayly by, and ſhoots beyond the view :
" Now to the Houſe of Sorrow urge thy way, *
" Whoſe darkſome round forbids the laughing day :
" As there thou ſhalt revolve the future ſcenes,
" While Fancy lifts the veil that intervenes,
" Let Hope celeſtial inmate of the heart,
" Her half-expanding proſpects ſtill impart :
" Think thro' the perils that encircling rear,
" I ſhall ſecurely urge my bold career,
" And at the cloſing of th' embattled ſtrife,
" Return perchance with fame-ennobled life,
" And fondly hanging on thy neck, recite
" The toil, the havock of the daring fight.

The fair return'd (with deep affliction fraught)
" When Gratitude firſt wak'd my infant thought,

* Antonio de Solis mentions in his hiſtory the Houſe of Mourning, which was frequented in the ſeaſon of calamity.

" And bade me raiſe it to th' auguſt abode,
" In thanks for ev'ry gift the God beſtow'd,
" In glowing thanks did I pour out my mind,
" That thou beſt gift was to my wiſh aſſign'd:
" Still with the fond expectancy elate
" Oft would my heart forerun the ling'ring date:
" Now as the Sun the ſplendid hour aſcends,
" Misfortune o'er the ſcene her cloud extends:
" Ah, GUATIMOZINO, what voice can tell
" The various ills that darken this farewell!
" Expos'd to peril, that enchanting form
" The thunder of the ſtranger may deform:
" Methinks I view thee in that blaſted ſtate,
" Dread ſpectacle—what horrours round thee wait?
" In vain theſe anxious eyes attempt to trace
" Ev'n the laſt ling'ring melancholy grace
" That death beſtows!"—Her voice now fails to flow,
Curs'd with the dire preſagement of her woe.
Behold, encircled by her virgin train,
The ſorrow-wedded fair forſakes the fane:

The parting fair the hero's eyes purſue,
While gliſten'd his young cheek with Pity's dew.

Lo, now commence the military rites,
While love of fame each panting breaſt excites.
Two youths, whom friendſhip and whom glory warms,
Come to demand the privilege of arms:
Beſide the ſtatue of the God they ſtand,
And rev'rent kiſs the darts that grace his hand:
Theſe ſacred darts the pow'r above beſtow'd,
A ſpirit bore them from the bright abode,
And in his paſſage to the ſphere below,
He dipt their plumage in the vernal bow.

See now at GUATIMOZINO's command,
To tuneful meaſures move the warlike band!
The ſquare encircling an extenſive plain,
Receives the patriot military train:
To them approach'd with ſpeedy march the foe,
While on each boſom valour pour'd a glow.

But chiefly GUATIMOZINO confeſs'd
The hero's feelings lab'ring in his breaſt:
There youthful Valour wak'd his ardent flame,
There breath'd contempt of death and love of fame,
There Intrepidity that ſcorns to ſtoop,
And ſoft-ey'd Clemency——enchanting group!
O'er theſe as Fancy ſtretch'd her brooding wing,
Preſcient ſhe ſaw, from this aſſortment, ſpring
Some great, ſhe knew not what, excelling deed,
That ſhou'd from Glory's hand obtain a meed.
Ev'n thus the bard who ſleeps near Avon's wave,
To whom the Muſe her unſunn'd treaſures gave,
When Genius ſmote him with his fierceſt beam,
And rous'd his boſom to ſome lofty theme,
His heart confeſs'd the ſomething yet unknown,
Which ſhou'd (to vigour's full perfection grown)
Riſe on the field of Poetry ſublime,
And brave invincible the ſcythe of Time.

Now from the bows the pointed weapons fly,
While from the foe the thund'ring tubes reply:

Of CORTEZ rushing on a fiery steed
The new-crown'd chieftain dares the course impede;
His eye illum'd with Valour's sparkling glance
Deep in the courser's chest he roots his lance;
But not his valour does the foe appall,
Still bleeding warriours round their hero fall.
Now to the lofty fane his troops repair,
Whose high ascending tow'rs are lost in air,
From whence the MEXICANS with speedy art
Show'r on the foe the death-inflicting dart:
Yet then by CORTEZ led, still undismay'd,
The SPANIARD host the lofty fane invade.

The two illustrious youths (whom Friendship's hand,
Had join'd with her indissoluble band)
Beheld indignant, smit with patriot grief,
The great achievements of the hostile chief:
And now JANELLAN thus accosts his friend:
" Firm to no purpose, active to no end,

" See from our gallant men yon hallow'd tow'r
" Already ravifh'd by th' invading pow'r:
" Muft this, committed to our mutual care,
" The fame defeat, the fame difhonour fhare?
" If fo——the victor fhall not long furvive—
" A thought that bids my fading hope revive:
" A thought—that like the thunder-flafh of night
" Darts on my darken'd mind a radiant light—
" But ere my veil'd defignment I unfold,
" Declare, however rafh, however bold,
" Thou'lt not o'erfhade with Caution's chill controul,
" The fplendid purpofe of my ardent foul."

VENZULA to his breaft his hand applied,
And thus beyond the pow'r of words replied.

The youth refum'd—" From this aerial height,
" Bid thy bold vifion take its deepeft flight,
" Down to yon rock, far ftretching o'er the fhore,
" 'Gainft which the raging waves inceffant roar,

" Whoſe claſhing voices into ſtillneſs fade,
" Ere this tremendous diſtance they pervade:
" If Fortune bleſs what my proud counſels urge,
" Yon waves ſhall murmur ſoon the victor's dirge!
" My ſecret project I will now unveil:
" Should CORTEZ o'er this valiant band prevail,
" Should thro' controlment, and thro' ſtubborn force,
" Pour like a torrent his deſtructive courſe,
" When on this ſummit firſt he ſhall appear,
" I will advance, with well-diſſembled fear,
" And, ſuppliant as I kneel to win his grace,
" I'll dauntleſs lock him in a ſtern embrace,
" Bear him reluctant to yon giddy ſteep,
" Where yawns a dreadful opening to the deep,
" And thence——ſelf-ruin'd for my country's good,
" Plunge with her foe into the whelming flood!"

VENZULA anſwered—" Yes, I much admire
" What now thy matchleſs virtue dares inſpire:

" But wilt thou, with an avarice of fame,
" The meed of Glory all exclufive claim?
" Wilt thou to perils clofe to Death adjoin'd
" Advance, and leave thy faithful friend behind?
" In infancy we fhar'd the glitt'ring toys,
" And in one circle play'd our harmlefs joys:
" And when we quitted childhood's lowly vale,
" Where fpringing flow'rets fcent the playful gale,
" Still hand in hand we climb'd youth's arduous height,
" Whence greater fcenes expanded on the fight,
" Still our purfuits confenting to one plan,
" Like wedded ftreams our lives united ran:
" And wilt thou now oppofe the facred tide,
" And bid the friendly waves difparting glide?"

JANELLAN fpoke—" Endearing youth forgive:
" The conq'ror of fome future CORTEZ live!
" Nor mark my fall with Grief's dejected brow,
" View from my death the bright effects that flow:

" Behold the tomb that Gratitude ſhall raiſe,
" Illuſtrious ſignal of my country's praiſe."

To this the brave VENZULA made reply,
And as he ſpoke, tears ſtarted from his eye:
" What tho' Felicity thy gift ſhall ſtream
" Sunlike o'er MEXICO with brighteſt beam,
" Not all the ſplendour that her rays impart,
" Will e'er illumine my benighted heart,
" When deſtitute of thee, its only ray,
" Without the hope of kind returning day."

" Thou beſt of friends, JANELLAN ſaid, ſuppreſs
" Of thy bright amity this warm exceſs,
" Leſt ſhrinking as it ſcorches I diſſolve,
" Unfram'd, unequal to my great reſolve!"

" Yet lend thine ear, VENZULA then rejoin'd,
" Sublimer motives urge my ſteady mind:

" Recall, recall that joy-diffusing hour,
" When gay Prosperity adorn'd my bow'r,
" As thy fair sister, half-afraid to speak,
" With down-cast look, and blush-embellish'd cheek,
" At Love's request assented to be mine:
" Of fleeting bliss vain momentary shine;
" For she, in flow'r of Youth and Virtue's bloom,
" Was swept untimely to the rav'nous tomb:
" As sorrow-wounded o'er her couch I hung,
" To catch the tones that faded as they sprung,
" *The God*, she said, *now summons me away,*
" *Far from the confines of th' endearing day:*
" *Thou of the life I lose the dearest part,*
" *Thou chosen spouse! thou sun-beam of my heart,*
" *Say, by Affection's glowing hand impress'd,*
" *Shall I not live in thy recording breast!*
" *If sacred be the suff'rer's last desires,*
" *Revere what now my parting soul requires:*
" *I leave a brother, by bright Honour rear'd,*
" *By all approv'd, and much to me endear'd:*

" *Be, for the ſiſter's love, the brother's friend;*
" *Nor from his ſide depart when ſtorms deſcend:*
" *The palm of Glory waving in your ſight,*
" *In council, peril, enterpriſe unite."*

" Shall I, when danger calls, conſign to air
" The laſt bequeathing wiſhes of the fair?
" Perdition catch the baſe unmanly thought!
" By Love's ſubliming pureſt dictates taught
" Amid the perils that around thee wait,
" View me reſolv'd to ſhare th' impending fate:
" Now to this ſpot the foe impels the war,
" Diſcordance ſcreams, oppoſing lances jar:
" The ſteep aſcent lo CORTEZ now has gain'd,
" Ah, mark his ſpear with ſtreaming gore diſtain'd.

Th' illuſtrious youths now act their dread deſign,
See at the victor's knee they low incline!
Now claſp with circling force th' incautious foe,
And cloſe adhering to his figure grow:

Their deadly aim his better fate controll'd,
With matchleſs pow'r he burſts their ſtubborn hold:
The heroes, blaſted in their bold intent,
Approach'd (Death hov'ring near) the dire deſcent:
Then, in each other's circling arms compreſs'd,
The laſt and dear farewell in ſighs expreſs'd:
'Twas Friendſhip burning with meridian flame,
One cauſe—one thought—one ruin—and one fame——
Tremendous moment! See, they fall from light,
And dauntleſs ruſh to never ending night!

Ye ſelf-devoted patriot victims, hail!
Oblivion's gulph ſhall ne'er entomb your tale:
While Hiſtory to Time's extremeſt goal
Her ſtream majeſtic ſhall thro' ages roll,
Like two fair flow'rets on one ſtem that blow
Ye on her margin ſhall for ever glow.*

* This ſublime inſtance of heroic Friendſhip is recorded by Antonio de Solis.

The royal youth, who ſaw th' aſpiring foe
The faint-oppoſing MEXICANS o'erthrow,
Felt (as he ſaw proud SPAIN's victorious ſcene)
The wound of Shame, the pointed ſhaft unſeen
That ſtings the heart: yet then to valour true,
The palm of Victory his thoughts purſue:
" Oh, youth of MEXICO, once valiant train,
" Raze from your radiant life this dark'ning ſtain:
" Say, ſhall the breaſts where Valour's flame ſhould burn,
" Your lifeleſs hearts as ſepulchres inurn?
" Thou weſtern Sun retard thy cloſing race,
" Nor to the Godhead witneſs our diſgrace:
" Our ſouls returning, a new conteſt claim,
" Still thy laſt ray ſhall on our honour flame."

The daring chief, with theſe exalting words,
Each ſlacken'd heart to Valour's tone accords:
And as a cloud by adverſe winds repell'd,
Returns full oft with double force impell'd,

Then ſailing pregnant with deſtructive ſtorms,
Diffuſes darkneſs, and the day deforms,
Till now deſcending with terrific roar,
Burſts from its womb the dire engender'd ſtore:
So, vengeance-ſtor'd, the fierce returning train
Impetuous ruſh upon the ſons of SPAIN;
Who ill the fierce deſtructive impulſe meet,
While terrour whiſpers to their ſouls——*retreat*:
That ignominious counſel they obey,
And urge precipitate their ſpeedy way.
The warm purſuit the MEXICANS releaſe,
Night ſpreads her ſtarry veil, and all is peace:
When ſudden from the tow'r's aſpiring height
The clarion * pierc'd the drowſy ear of night;
That ſacred inſtrument! whoſe voice renown'd
Yields rarely to the world its tone profound:
TALEPO breathing thro' its brazen throat,
Diffus'd around a deep-inſpiring note,

* The MEXICAN Hiſtorian takes notice of the *ſacred Trumpet.* It was not permitted to any but the prieſts to ſound it; and that only when they animated the people on the part of their Gods.

While on each youthful valour-heaving breaſt
Religion her warm energy impreſs'd:
Now tenfold rage impels the martial train,
While leaps the pulſe thro' ev'ry ardent vein:
Fierce they purſue the fleeting SPANIARD hoſt,
Who from the neighbouring lake's projected coaſt,
Ruſh down (as on their prey the Falcons dart)
And truſt to ſafety from their buoyant art:
Vain hope! ſee at the royal chief's command
Of dauntleſs MEXICANS a choſen band,
Prompt as the quickneſs of the lightning's gleam,
Plunge with their leader in the roaring ſtream:
With one bold arm thro' clam'rous waves they ſteer,
With one they raiſe aloft the threat'ning ſpear:
Thus vehement they urge the hoſtile train,
Inflicting vengeance on the ſons of SPAIN,
Ev'n till the wide-diffuſing drops of blood
Spread like a ſcarlet mantle o'er the flood.

Of MEXICO the Genius now deſcends,
And near the angry waters as he bends,

The cryſtal goblet that his hands ſuſtain,
He plunges thrice into the tinctur'd main!
Then ſoars, and on the neighb'ring mountain's height,
The radiant pow'r arreſts his rapid flight,
Where in full conclave a terrific band,
The ſpirits of illuſtrious chieftains ſtand!—
Not with the patriot does his paſſion die,
It breathes—'tis Immortality's ally:
Still from the tomb the warm affections flow
Ev'n as the ſunſet-ſky retains a glow.

" Mark, mark, the Genius ſaid, this precious vaſe,
" Here pleas'd affix, here feaſt your raptur'd gaze:
" The vaſt canal near Mexico that flows,
" Aſſumes the colour that this cryſtal ſhows:
" Its ſwelling ſurges daſh the ſounding ſhore,
" Inflam'd and crimſon'd with the hoſtile gore."

Touch'd at the welcome tidings they rejoice,
And to the gale commit their feeble voice:

Lo, now diſburden'd of their preſſing care,
They tow'r aloft, and vaniſh into air.

Tho' Victory her ſun-bright glory ſhed
Full and unſullied round the hero's head,
At Nature's voice he checks the ſmile of Joy,
And fun'ral duties now his thoughts employ:
The death-ground opening its capacious womb
Receives the dread depoſite in its gloom.
Now, with uneven, but perſuaſive ſtrains,
To wake the boſom, Harmony complains,
While Joy, obedient to the magic lay,
Diſſolves like ſnow before the melting ray:
Now fades th' expiring ſweetly plaintive ſound,
While ſtill as midnight, Silence reigns around:
Chain'd is each voice, while o'er the awe-ſtruck ſenſe
Diſtill the ſober horrours of ſuſpenſe:
At length the chief th' expecting ſilence broke,
While pointing to the patriot tomb, he ſpoke:

" Hail, ſepulchre, which ev'ry coward ſhuns!
" Thou glorious hecatomb of Valour's ſons!
" On thee, oh ſacred altar of renown,
" Th' eternal being looks propitious down!
" They, they are dear to that all-ſeeing eye,
" Who greatly daring act, or bravely die.
" Let this ſuggeſtion ſoothe the bleeding heart,
" In which deſpair has lodg'd his poiſon'd dart:
" To you I ſpeak, ye fair afflicted train,
" Who weep for brothers, friends, and lovers ſlain:
" To you I ſpeak, ye widows plung'd in care;
" And you whoſe ſons ſtern fate refus'd to ſpare.

As thus he ſaid—deep from ſome breaſt unknown,
Burſt unſubdued Affliction's piercing moan,
Now intermitting, now returning loud—
At length, advancing thro' the wond'ring crowd,
A matron-form th' attentive hero view'd,
Her robe neglected, and her treſſes rude,

With hurried ſtep the royal youth ſhe ſought,
Her wild eye ſpeaking th' inexpreſſive thought:
Cloſe at her ſide a lovely boy appears——
Now through oppoſing grief her voice ſhe tears:
" Give, give to me, the virtue that repels,
" The whelming ſurge of Sorrow at it ſwells:
" Two valiant ſons, in age my comfort's ſtore,
" My lov'd, my duteous children, are no more:
" This morn, this direful morn, a prey to fears,
" I bath'd our parting with preſaging tears:
" That they expir'd on Honour's ſacred bed,
" That their ſouls mingle with th' illuſtrious dead,
" Well do I know—and glory in the thought:
" Bright Virtue's flame, perchance, from me they caught,
" From me th' inſtructive leſſon firſt they claim'd,
" This boſom nurtur'd, and this voice inflam'd.
" Yet ill with this vain pomp of ſplendid words,
" My drooping, loaded, ſinking heart accords:
" Ah, ſtill to Glory's thought deſpair ſucceeds,
" And th' agonizing mother inly bleeds.

" This orphan babe to you I now bequeathe,
" With Honour's brighteſt flow'rs his mind inwreathe."

The child, half-conſcious of the mother's grief,
As if attempting to diſpenſe relief,
Stretch'd forth his little arms, and playful ſmil'd.
In vain the boy her ſcorpion thoughts beguil'd,
Inclining at his call her anguiſh'd face,
Death-ſtruck ſhe periſh'd in the wiſh'd embrace.

'Twas then the hero thus his thoughts expreſs'd:
" Fly, wounded ſpirit, to the realms of reſt!
" This orphan child committed to my care,
" This tender object of thy cloſing pray'r,
" The blood that warms his breaſt, his helpleſs years,
" But moſt thy laſt requeſt, to me endears."

The hero added—" Shall the captive train
" Partake the fate the rigid laws ordain?
" As erring friends 'tis virtuous to forgive,
" 'Tis godlike to decree the foe to live!

" Ah then, while Pity does her thoughts ſuggeſt,
" We feel the glowing God within our breaſt.
" Amid the captives one ſuperiour moves,
" Whoſe gen'rous deeds humanity approves,
" One whoſe pure boſom all the Virtues claim,
" Reſpectful man! LAS CASAS is his name:
" He for Religion's ſake Religion woo'd,
" Warm at her ſhrine the prieſt enamour'd ſtood:
" When cruel Havock bade the war encreaſe,
" Still o'er the plain he ſtrew'd the flow'rs of Peace:
" To ſoothe the proſtrate foe his wiſdom plann'd,
" While hover'd o'er the wound his healing hand:
" Yet not to theſe endearing acts confin'd,
" He pour'd the balm of comfort on the mind:
" Let then the ſacred prieſt your friendſhip ſhare,
" And at his voice the death-doom'd captives ſpare."
He ſaid—and to the God of war ordain'd
A ſpotleſs rite by human gore unſtain'd.*

* See the character of this SPANISH Biſhop, ſo celebrated for his humanity, as it is drawn by the maſterly hand of the Abbé RAYNAL in the third volume of his *Hiſtoire philoſophique et politique.*

Now, ſee the hero with the wedded fair,
(While ſportive Fancy runs before) repair,
By Truth conducted to the dim alcove,
Where Pleaſure rears the roſy couch of Love.

TALEPO now the Chriſtian prieſt addreſs'd:
" While Silence lulls the drooping world to reſt,
" Let us enjoy the conf'rence of an hour
" Within the boſom of this ſecret bow'r:
" Say, 'mid the ſpoilers of this peaceful land,
" That rude unfeeling, bold deſtructive band,
" Who their baſe hands in guiltleſs blood imbrue,
" Oh, prieſt of meekneſs, what had'ſt thou to do?
" Say, of your country thus inur'd to fight,
" Do all in ſtrife and maſſacres delight?
" Say, to what rigid Deity ye bend,
" If thro' our woes your pray'rs approv'd aſcend?

LAS CASAS ſpoke——" Compell'd to join the hoſt,
" Reluctantly I ſought your peaceful coaſt:

" Nor of my country, with inhuman joy,
" Do all uplift their weapons to deſtroy:
" Nor is the Deity to whom we bow,
" Such as your vague bewild'ring thoughts avow:
" Indignant He beheld the martial train,
" With bloody purpoſe ruſhing o'er the main:
" Ill we deſerve the bleſſings he beſtow'd:
" For us he quitted the divine abode—
" As on the humble earth with man He trod
" Thro' all her works aw'd Nature own'd her God.
" The palſied ſuff'rer left his weary bed,
" While on his cheek Health's brighteſt colour bled:
" And ſtranger ſtill—the tenant of the tomb,
" Who long had dwelt in Death's relentleſs womb,
" Upborn abruptly from the yawning ground,
" Amazement-ſmitten caſt his eyes around!"

" Ah, highly favour'd race, TALÈPO cried,
" Say, wherefore was your bliſs to us denied?

" God of the Chriſtians, ſpeak the crime unknown
" For which an hoſt of Virtues can't atone!
" For which proſcrib'd, diſgrac'd, this hapleſs coaſt
" Is raviſh'd of thoſe gifts your children boaſt!
" Ah now, Las Casas, haſten to relate,
" The bright effects of your exalted ſtate,
" The fruits that ripen from celeſtial ſeeds!
" Heroic thoughts! and burſt of glorious deeds!
" You pauſe—what means that ſorrow-ſhaded eye?
" That fix'd reluctance, that betraying ſigh?

" Forbear, the prieſt return'd, thy vain requeſt,
" Nor call the truth from this unwilling breaſt:
" Tho' many godlike deeds our faith endear,
" The Chriſtian ſtory blaſts th' expecting ear.
" The Godhead ſpoke—*Let Meekneſs as a dove*
" *Brood in man's heart the ſacred acts of Love.*
" But mark the ſtrange reſult——in hoſtile bands
" The Chriſtians hurry to remoter lands,

" To Death consigning, deaf to Pity's claim,
" The realms unknowing of their founder's name.
" From these dire acts they rouz'd to new alarms,
" And on each other turn'd their reeking arms.
" The gen'ral Faith receiv'd Destruction's shock,
" And as a vessel dash'd against a rock,
" Was split into a thousand jarring creeds,
" Each breathing rage and sanguinary deeds.
" Then Persecution wak'd the Martyr's pile,
" And hail'd the sparkles with a greedy smile."

TALEPO said—" The creed of distant tribes,
" From your high-favour'd realm remote, imbibes
" No knowledge of your God.—Ah, tell me true,
" Bright Virtue's path do we in vain pursue?
" Say, do we nurse with ineffectual care
" The hope which soothes the pain that all must bear,
" Who speaks of bliss beyond this lower sphere,
" And whispers comfort to the dying ear?"

"Thrice virtuous ſage, the feeling prieſt rejoin'd,
"Ah let not doubt o'erſhade thy ſpotleſs mind:
"The diff'rent tenets that each nation claims—
"To heav'nly pow'r affix'd the various names—
"Are as the rays projecting from the ſun!
"Are but the titles of th' Eternal One!
"The many modes of worſhip, as they tend
"To one refining pure celeſtial end,
"Ev'n from that, diverſe homage may aſpire
"A grateful off'ring to th' immortal Sire,
"As from the flow'rs of variegated dies
"Exhales a blended incenſe to the ſkies.
"On us with energy the Godhead beams,
"And on thy valiant clime but faintly gleams,
"Yet be not thou diſturb'd, nor fear to ſtray
"In queſt of Virtue far from Virtue's way:
"As round his little path, tho' gloom'd by night,
"The radiant inſect throws a guiding light;
"So all unerring ſee to act their part,
"Taught by the glitt'ring glow-worm of the heart."

Talepo now, to bright conviction won,
Exclaim'd, enchanted, " Oh thou better Sun!
" Thy words like dayſpring on the breaſt of night,
" Pour on my darken'd ſoul th' endearing light—
" But partial light, for ſtill within the mind
" Full many a painful doubt remains behind.
" What is that pow'r we Chance or Fortune call,
" Who holds her veering miniſtry o'er all,
" Reſembling ſtill that ſpirit of the ſky,
" Whoſe ſecret form eludes the human eye;
" Who now unmindful of its matchleſs pow'r
" Indulgent whiſpers to the vernal flow'r,
" Plays with her leaves, and hov'ring o'er her bloom
" From her young breaſt allures the enclos'd perfume:
" And now envelop'd in a ſullen mood,
" Tempeſtuous ruſhes on the groaning wood,
" Arm'd with deſtructive energy, invades,
" Deſpoils, devaſts the conſecrated ſhades.

" Still with the cloud of Ignorance oppreſs'd,
" Enlighten'd prieſt, unfold to my requeſt,
" Of dire Neceſſity the hidden cauſe,
" Who ſeems on Freedom's ground to fix her laws,
" And combats and diſtracts the human will,
" As the wild ſtorm confounds the pilot's ſkill.

" Tell, if thou can'ſt, what pow'r impels the mind,
" When, loth in narrow bounds to be confin'd,
" She breaks diſdainful from her native ſphere,
" And ſoars exulting in a new career:
" And in her progreſs ſends a daring glance
" Along Futurity's opaque expanſe,
" That dread depoſitory, veil'd abode,
" Where breathe the ſecret counſels of the God!

" Still in my ſoul perplexing doubts remain,
" All knowing ſage, that radiant pow'r explain,
" Who when the world with low'ring clouds is hung,
" Darts like the ſun from his high orbit flung,

" And wing'd with ſwiftneſs, wild diſtracted flies,
" Diſperſing terrour thro' the conſcious ſkies:
" Then the tremendous voice that ſpeaks on high,
" As if ſome angry God bade Nature die."

Thus thro' their converſe ſtole with magic pow'r,
All unobſerv'd, the ſlow nocturnal hour;
Till, as the ſhades forſook the morning ſky,
The God of day diſclos'd his radiant eye,
Which dropping luſtre on the conſcious main,
Shew'd to the deep-deſponding ſons of SPAIN,
A kindred fleet by urging zephyrs fann'd,
Triumphant ſailing to th' impatient ſtrand.
Rich tablature! by Expectation glaz'd,
By Hope high-colour'd, and by Joy emblaz'd.
See CORTEZ now, emerging from deſpair,
For all the butchery of war prepare;
Revenge and Maſſacre, the ſaints that crown
The bloody altar of his baſe renown,

Now goad him on to ſnatch the wealthy prize,
Whoſe golden treaſures glitter in his eyes.
Meanwhile Deſpondence (like approaching night)
Of INDIAN valour dims the ſplendid light;
O'er MEXICANS her fenny pinions ſpreads,
And on their boſoms chilling fear-drops ſheds.
To raiſe their drooping ſoul the chief compels
The magic ſeers to quit their lonely cells:
Three awful forms appear—in white array'd,
Whoſe rev'rend temples ſilver treſſes ſhade.
To them TALEPO—" If your hallow'd mind,
" As Fame reports by Wiſdom's ray refin'd,
" Can glance into Futurity's contents,
" And wander forth to meet the great events
" At diſtance ſailing thro' their long career,
" To take their ſtation in this lower ſphere!
" Then ſpeak our fate—does Ruin hover near?
" And do we vainly graſp the hoſtile ſpear?"

DRACONO ſpoke—" Thy wond'ring viſion raiſe,
" And mark yon angry comet's threat'ning blaze!
" Haſt thou not heard loud howlings of deſpair,
" And ſhrieks of horrour vex the midnight air?
" The dreaded pow'r, who from his baleful breath
" Sends pains, ſends peſtilence, and ſudden death,
" Amid the terrours of the conſcious night,
" That God malignant ruſh'd upon my ſight:
" *Advert to* MEXICO'*s diſtreſsful ſtate,*
" *Behold the future picture of her fate.*
He ſaid—when lo a low'ring cloud o'erſpread
" And mantled MEXICO's imperial head:
" Tall columns of dun ſmoke encircling join'd,
" Which wreaths of flame like angry ſnakes entwin'd."

" Peace, terrour-ſpreading prieſt, the chief replied,
" Think not my people in your voice confide:
" Well I recall, how, in my early youth,
" Your dark predictions wander'd far from truth:

" The mid-day sun recoil'd, involv'd in night,
" While thou, the pander to the gen'ral fright,
" Did'st dastard-like thy voice prophetic rear,
" And loud assert—*The death of Time was near,*
" *That at her flood-gates stood Destruction's pow'r*
" *To deluge Nature in a fiery show'r.*"

" The trembling world the chain of Silence bound,
" While dreadful Expectation hover'd round:
" When from his cloud emerg'd the God of day,
" And nature burst into a grateful lay:
" So from the low'ring cloud of our distress
" May dart the glorious sun-beams of Success.
" To war, to war let us again resort,
" And Victory by deeds of valour court."
He added not—but hast'ning to the shore,
He bade his warriours grasp the guiding oar,
Determin'd on the bosom of the main
To dare the proud augmented pow'r of SPAIN,

Whoſe ſtately brigantines, with ſpreading ſail,
Approach obedient to the ſullen gale,
Which like a miſchief-urging ſpirit guides
The hoſtile veſſels o'er the rolling tides:
With ruin fraught the vaſt progreſſive ſcene
Diſparting——leaves a dreadful ſpace between.
To this dread ſpace to war the ſtronger foe,
The daring chief directs his light canoe:
So mariners have ſeen the Sword-fiſh ſail
With bold intent to wound the giant Whale.
Now SPANISH art unlocks her deathful ſtore,
While on the gallies burſts Deſtruction's roar.
Dark o'er the ſcene impends a veil of ſmoke,
By frequent flaſhes of the cannon broke.

'Twas then Fatality, myſterious queen,
Who reigns deſpotic o'er this lower ſcene,
Unqueſtion'd guides the riſe and fall of realms,
An empire now exalts, and now o'erwhelms,

Beheld her prieſteſs, Revolution, ſtand!
Prompt on the myſtic wheel to lay her hand:
" Urge, urge thy taſk, the fatal Goddeſs ſaid,
" For MEXICO muſt bend her regal head."
The myſtic wheel performs th' appointed round,
And mark the chief in chains diſgraceful bound:
Ah, ſee the youth approach the crowded ſhore,
While from the foe aſcends th' applauding roar.
Now to the royal dome his ſteps he bends,
So lately peopled with his valiant friends:
There, there, oh ſight accurs'd, in evil hour
He views proud CORTEZ on the ſeat of pow'r:
Who meanly vain, thus loud inſulting ſaid,
" Is all thy courage and reſiſtance dead?
" The loyal troops that tread thy ſubject plains,
" Do they conſent to view their king in chains?
" Audacious MEXICAN, behold how vain
" To war againſt th' uplifted arm of SPAIN!

" Beneath yon plains, in ſome ſequeſter'd ſcene,
" Well do I know that Nature works unſeen,
" Forms with creative hand the buried ore,
" To you an uſeleſs and unheeded ſtore :
" Does ſtrong deſire ſtill prompt thy heart to live,
" Then give to my impatient ſight, oh give !
" The cunning artiſt at her ſecret toil,
" And glut my wiſhes with the glitt'ring ſpoil !"

The captive hero gave theſe words to flow
(While his eye flaſh'd defiance on the foe)
" Theſe chains but only reach th' exterior form,
" The bulwark of the mind thou can'ſt not ſtorm :
" Misjudging man ! think not thy proud control,
" Tho' all around your boaſted thunders roll,
" Can e'er invade the temple of the Soul ;
" There lives the ſecret that thou woud'ſt devour,
" And laughs at thy vain impotence of pow'r."

" Still ſhall thy haughtineſs be taught to crouch,
" The victor ſaid—Prepare the fiery couch,
" Pile glowing torches on th' extended frame,
" And clothe it with a robe of raging flame."

Yet unappall'd the godlike youth rejoin'd:
" If thro' the night of thine umbrageous mind,
" Could radiant mercy dart a cheering ray,
" And melt to ſoftneſs thy tyrannic ſway,
" To thy diſtinction would I then confide
" That youthful captive, to my blood allied:
" Ah, on that venerable grief-ſtruck ſage
" Look down, and ſmooth the rugged path of age.
" But moſt relenting to this mourner bend,
" And o'er her days thy guardian care extend."
He ceas'd—and turning to the drooping fair,
Who ſtood a monument of dumb Deſpair;
While Sorrow's iron hand her boſom wrung,
He on her neck in mournful ſilence hung.

Now from the chains that frame this fond delay,
Victorious o'er himfelf he breaks away,
And now advances, by rude ruffians led,
With ftep undaunted, to the tort'ring bed:
Alarm'd to meet his kindred warriour there—
" Oh thou, he faid, who did'ft the battle fhare,
" Muft thou, unhappy youth, endure with me
" This laft fevere refult of SPAIN's decree?
" Then raife thy heart fuperiour to the tafk,
" Nor fear beneath thofe tranfient flames to bafk;
" Ev'n ere they fade th' immortal Soul fhall rife,
" And take its feat of blifs in yonder fkies,
" Where to thy wond'ring vifion fhall expand,
" Adorn'd with heroes, a refulgent land,
" Where valiant MEXICANS, fecure from woe,
" Look down contemptuous on the SPANISH foe."

He faid—and to his rigid doom refign'd,
Along the flaming couch his form reclin'd:

The partner of his fate ſubmiſſive bends,
And o'er the tort'ring bed his frame extends;
Yet then unequal to the conq'ring pain,
He ſpoke his ſuff'ring in lamenting ſtrain:
" O, royal maſter, give me to diſcloſe
" Where in the mine the golden treaſure glows—
" I ſhrink, I faint, inferiour to my part,
" And this frail frame betrays my daring heart."

Amidſt the raging flames that round him blaz'd,
The royal chief his martyr'd figure rais'd,
Caſt on the youth a calm-reproaching eye,
And ſpoke—oh eloquent, ſublime reply!
Oh heav'n! oh earth! attend
" Do I REPOSE
" ALL ON THE SILKEN FOLIAGE OF THE ROSE?"
He ceas'd—and deep within his ſoul retir'd,
To honour firm, triumphant he expir'd.

Thy arduous taſk, brave youth, thou'ſt well perform'd,
Tho' perils, threats, and tortures round thee ſtorm'd:

O'er thy laſt ſcene admiring angels hung,
And at thy exit lound applauding ſung:
Thy ſpirit glowing with celeſtial fire,
To Heav'n is wafted by th' angelic 'quire:
The gorgeous ſpectacle aſcending high,
Sails thro' the portal of the parting ſky,
And at the living throne arreſts its flight,
O'er which is ſpread a brilliant flood of light;
There the dread preſence dwells in deep receſs,
Encompaſs'd round with Glory's rich exceſs.
Now, thro' the veil of bright redundant beams,
A voice is heard—"' From me Creation ſtreams—
"' I am the Pow'r—I from th' entombing Earth
"' Exalt the virtuous to a ſecond Birth;
"' To them delighted I diſcloſe the ray
"' Of Immortality's long Summer Day.'"

But ſee TALEPO, venerable ſeer,
Approach the ſcene, impreſs'd with buſy fear,

When firſt th' inhuman deed appall'd his ſight
Ev'n as the cedar ſhrunk in ſudden blight
He ſtood—while at the dire appearance thrill'd,
Each function of the ſoul ſtiff Horrour chill'd:
At length relenting into conſcious grief,
He loud exclaim'd—" Oh lov'd, oh hapleſs chief!
" The aſhes ſtill that feed yon ling'ring flame,
" Do they of all thou art th' exiſtence claim?
" Long ſchool'd in pale Adverſity's rude porch,
" Where Hope's gay domes are burnt by Havock's torch,
" For me, with grief adjoin'd to age oppreſs'd,
" Remain'd but this to cleave my care-worn breaſt.
" In early youth to me thou waſt conſign'd,
" I watch'd the dawn of thy celeſtial mind,
" I ſaw, by Nature wak'd, thy talents riſe,
" And Virtue mark them with her brighteſt dies.
" Ah what avail theſe fruitleſs tears I ſhed?
" Tho' thou art gone—yet Vengeance is not dead:
" The pregnant womb of Time"—He added not—
While from his eye a radiant meaning ſhot.

His boſom heav'd with a prophetic throe,
Till language gave his ſtruggling thoughts to flow.

"Methinks Futurity, celeſtial maid,
" Thro' diſtant Time's dim length'ning iſle diſplay'd,
" Pours on my favour'd viſion days unborn,
" That pant impatient for the ling'ring morn:
" Smooth as the clear expanſe of vernal ſkies,
" A world of water claims my wond'ring eyes,
" See on its wavy breaſt, in ſplendid pride,
" Innum'rous brigantines triumphant ride: *
" Mark how the gorgeous maſs advancing ploughs
" The groaning main with high aſpiring prows:
" Secure in all the haughtineſs of ſtrength,
" It moves a creſcent of tremendous length,
" And big with thunders and deſtructive force,
" To BRITAIN's coaſt directs its threat'ning courſe.

* The SPANISH Armada ſailed in 1588, *diſpoſed in the form of a creſcent, and ſtretching the diſtance of ſeven miles from the extremity of one diviſion to that of the other.*

HUME.

" Oft has LAS CASAS, in applauding ſtrain,
" To me reveal'd that ſea-encircled plain.
" Thou Glory of the Weſt! inchanted iſle,
" Where beauteous maids on godlike heroes ſmile:
" By Nature's hand with Nature's chaplet crown'd
" In arts, in commerce, and in arms renown'd;
" Auguſt, magnificent, exalted Dame,
" As with a garment rob'd in Freedom's flame!
" Ariſe, ariſe—foreſtall th' intended blow,
" See to thy portal ſails th' audacious foe.

" Another ſcenery is now diſplay'd
" No more the main aſſembled veſſels ſhade,
" A beggar'd remnant (of the ſplendid throng
" That ſwept in conſcious majeſty along)
" With prows disfigur'd, and diſhonour'd maſts,
" While thro' the rent ſails mourn the hollow blaſts,
" In ſhatter'd, mean, diſmantled rude array,
" Steal o'er the waves their ignominious way.

" Oh of thy brilliant and extenſive train
" Do theſe, ARMADA, theſe alone remain?
" Who has o'erthrown the honours of thy helm?
" The voice of Fame replies——ELIZA's realm!
" Where lurk thy galleons that ſurpris'd the deep?
" Loud Fame replies——in Ocean's tomb they ſleep!
" And of HISPANIA once the bright renown,
" Now glows an added gem to BRITAIN's crown.

" Enough—enough, ſubmiſſive to my fate
" I now return to my diſtreſsful ſtate:
" Thanks to the God, whoſe kind revealing pow'r
" Gilds with a chearful ray my cloſing hour."

THE

VENETIAN MARRIAGE,

BY THE SAME.

THE

VENETIAN MARRIAGE.

THE weſtern ſun's expiring ray
To VENICE gave a milder day;
Till by degrees the ling'ring light
Hung trembling on the verge of night.
CAMILLA then, with fearful ſoul,
To th' Adriatic margin ſtole,
Where in a bark, at Love's command,
PLACENTIO took his faithful ſtand.
Poſſeſſing now his future bride,
He bade the bark ſecurely glide,
Which far unlike that gally ſhow'd
That down the ſilver Cydnus row'd,

Beneath whoſe purple ſails were ſeen,
Proud Oſtentation's gaudy Queen,
Who ſure of conqueſt, vain of mind,
All languiſhingly lay reclined!
Here Beauty undefil'd by art,
Whoſe boſom own'd a tender heart,
Beneath the ſails from home remov'd,
And truſted to the man ſhe lov'd.

A vernal calmneſs lull'd the deep,
And huſh'd each wavy ſurge to ſleep:
The air along the ſultry day,
Scorch'd by the Summer's fervent ray,
Was freſhen'd by a recent ſhow'r,
While Silence ſolemniz'd the hour.

The ſtill ſolemnity impreſs'd
With awful thought's CAMILLA's breaſt,
For now by prompting Love impell'd,
Now by Timidity witheld,

The words which to pronounce ſhe tried,
Recoil'd, and unaccented died.
PLACENTO too alike ſubdued,
They ſail'd along in ſilent mood,
And ſtillneſs reign'd from ſhore to ſhore,
Unbroke——but by the daſhing oar.

At length the fair diſſolv'd the charm—
" Ah, wonder not I feel alarm!
" Confiding in thy love I came,
" And riſk'd for thee my virgin fame:
" Ah tell me to what place we ſail,
" For in my boſom fears prevail:
" Yet anſwer not this idle fear,
" Where'er thou art bright honour's there."

" The plan I form, the youth replied,
" To Innocence is cloſe allied,
" And fearful of thy virgin fame
" As of her babe the tender dame.

" Theſe waves that wander to the ſea,
" Waſh in their pilgrimage a tree,
" Which ſpreads its lowly branches wide,
" And dips them in the paſſing tide:
" There, in a ſhade compos'd of reeds,
" An aged hermit tells his beads:
" He, gen'rous ſage, will join our hands
" In wedlock's unremitting bands.
" Then to VALCLUSA we'll repair,
" Where LAURA's ſoul informs the air:
" Where PETRARCH's ſpirit hovers round,
" The guardian of the ſacred ground,
" Forbidding ſtill that fiend of art,
" That ſhrewd perverter of the heart,
" The ſnake, Inconſtancy, to rove
" Within the paradiſe of Love.

" As when chill Winter quits the land,
" The ſnow-drop does her leaves expand,

" So may chill fears your breaſt releaſe,
" Till gently it expands to peace,
" Mild as theſe twilight breezes blow,
" Soft as the waves on which we flow."

" Ye walls where firſt I drew the air,
" Return'd (aſſur'd) the beauteous fair;
" Ye turrets which but dimly ſeen
" Encreaſe the terrour of the ſcene!
" Ye ſtately tow'rs! and riſing ſpires!
" From you CAMILLA now retires.
" Thou tomb whoſe pious urn contains
" My ſacred parents' cold remains!
" Ye partners of my tender years,
" Whom youthful ſympathy endears:
" Ye joys that crown my native coaſt,
" Well for PLACENTIO all are loſt."

She ceas'd—and on her penſive ſoul
Again an awful muſing ſtole,

Such as the twilight ſcene excites,
Such as the feeling heart delights;
For as the coy nocturnal flow'r
No more its ſweets at eve witholds,
So the meek heart at th' evening hour
Its ſenſibility unfolds.

See now they reach the ſacred cell
Where Wiſdom, Peace, and Virtue dwell:
There, bent beneath the weight of age,
They find prepar'd th' expecting ſage.
He hail'd them in a friendly tone,
And bade them call his cell their own:
Where roſe an altar form'd of moſs,
Crown'd with a ſimple wooden croſs!
There too a taper, mildly bright,
Supplied a pompous glare of light:
No holy relick rich-enchas'd
This unambitious altar grac'd:

Here Flora, Nature's prieſteſs, ſtood,
And round her fragrant off'rings ſtrew'd.

The hermit ſpoke—" Hail, virtuous pair,
" May your misfortunes periſh here:
" Tho' youth be yours, yet well I know
" You've taſted deep of human woe!
" Control, and art, and baſeneſs join'd,
" To cancel what your hearts deſign'd:
" But now Misfortune's reign is o'er,
" And Pleaſure opens all her ſtore."

He paus'd—and now the youthful pair
Th' irrevocable vow prefer:
And now the hermit clos'd their hands
In willing and unvenal bands,
Unſpotted bands! which mutual Love,
And Confidence and Virtue wove.

F I N I S.

www.ingramcontent.com/pod-product-compliance
Lightning Source LLC
Chambersburg PA
CBHW021226260626
47172CB00002B/629
9783744712668